Passover

Festivals and Holidays

By June Behrens

Photographs Compiled by Terry Behrens

CHILDRENS PRESS ®

CHICAGO

TO RUTH ADLER SNAVELY

ACKNOWLEDGMENTS

The author wishes to acknowledge the assistance of Rabbi David Lieb of Temple Beth El in San Pedro, California.

A special thanks to members of the Pollack family—Stephen and Judy, their daughters Jennifer and Sara, and grandparents Tiby and Ted Goldstein.

Others who helped by serving as photographer's models and assistants include Michael and Dee Fishman, Andrea Hannon, and Pauline Brower.

PHOTO CREDITS

Cover: The family celebrating Passover.

Back Cover: A velvet matzo cloth decorated with silk and metallic threads, shells, and sequins (from the Hebrew Union College Skirball Museum).

The author also wishes to thank Susanne Kester and the Hebrew Union College Skirball Museum for the photographs that appear on pages 18, 32, and the back cover.

Library of Congress Cataloging in Publication Data

Behrens, June.
  Passover: the festival of freedom.

  (Ethnic and traditional holidays)
  Summary: Follows the members of the Adler family as they prepare for and celebrate Passover.
  1. Passover—Juvenile literature. [1. Passover]
I. Behrens, Terry, ill. II. Title. III. Series.
BM695.P3B39 1987   296.4'37   87-5161
ISBN 0-516-02389-6

Passover

On the night before Passover, Mr. Adler and the children search the house to sweep it clean of all foods made with yeast. These are forbidden foods—*hametz*.

PASSOVER
The Festival of Freedom

"I found it. I found a crumb of *hametz*! Where is our candy?" asks Ruthie. Father holds the candle while Ruthie sweeps the crumbs into the dustpan Sara is holding.

It is the night before the Passover holiday. Ruthie, Sara, and Nathan are playing a game that is a tradition in the Adler family. They carry a candle, a feather, and a dustpan. They search the house and sweep it clean of anything baked with yeast.

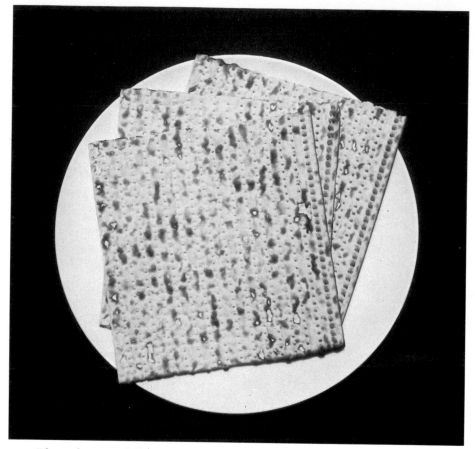

The unleavened flat bread called matzo is eaten during Passover.

These foods, called *hametz*, include bread and cereals, spaghetti, and crackers. These are forbidden foods. Thin pieces of unleavened flat bread called matzo are eaten during Passover. Only flourlike matzo meal and potato starch are used in cooking during this holiday.

The children search for *hametz* crumbs, as well as for the candy Father has hidden. The game reminds them of the Jews who for hundreds of years have searched their homes for *hametz* the night before Passover. Grandfather watches as the children find their *hametz* candy under a sofa cushion.

Grandfather looks up from his paper to watch the children find the *hametz* candy their father has hidden. This is the last *hametz* they will eat until Passover ends.

Passover is a very important holiday for the Adlers. This festival of freedom is celebrated by Jewish families all over the world. Passover retells their story of freedom from slavery in Egypt over three thousand years ago.

In spring the Adler family celebrates Passover for seven days. Other Jewish families might celebrate for eight days, depending on the family custom. Ruthie and Sara help Mrs. Adler clean the house and wash the windows. All the kitchenware used daily is put away. A special set of kitchen utensils and dishes is used to prepare and serve the Passover meals. Forbidden foods are removed from the kitchen.

Everyone helps prepare the house for Passover. Everything must be clean and fresh for the holiday.

Mrs. Adler buys the different foods and the wine needed for the holiday. Food is an important part of the Passover celebration. She takes the children shopping for new clothes. Everything must be bright and new and clean for this important festival.

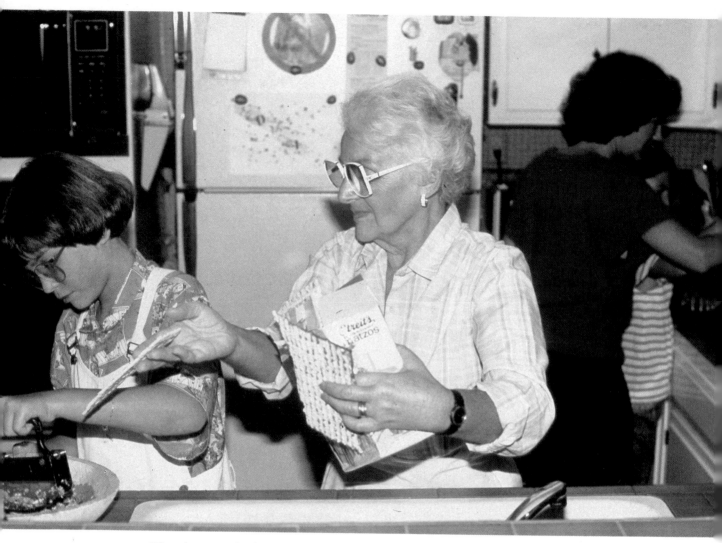

Oh, what wonderful smells! The kitchen is a busy place as the special Passover foods are prepared.

Ruthie and Sara help mother with the cooking. Grandmother makes a special Passover dish. The kitchen is a busy place the day before Passover.

Ruthie and Sara set the table with
their best Passover dishes and linens.
Each setting will have a wine glass. It is
a beautiful, festive table.

The table gleams with the family's best Passover silver, china, and
glassware. The tablecloth is sparkling white. Everything looks
beautiful.

Grandfather reads the story of the first Passover. They have heard the story before, but they enjoy hearing it every year. Having Grandfather read the story of Passover is part of the Adler family traditions.

Passover centers around the home, the family, and food. The celebration helps to keep the Adler family customs and religious traditions alive. The holiday begins on the fifteenth day of the Jewish month of Nisan.

Grandfather tells the children that the Hebrew word for Passover is *Pesah*. It means "passing over." The first Passover story is told in Exodus, a book in the Old Testament of the Bible.

Grandfather reads about how the Jews left their land and moved to Egypt more than three thousand years ago. For a time they lived in harmony with the people there. After many years a cruel ruler came into power. The Jews were forced into slavery. They worked to build the temples and cities of this Egyptian ruler, called the Pharaoh.

Here Moses is shown asking the Pharaoh to let the Jews leave Egypt. The Pharaoh says no.

Moses, the leader of the Jews, asked the Pharaoh to let his people go. The Jews wanted to return to their homeland in Canaan, also called Israel. The Pharaoh would not let them go.

16

Great disasters, called plagues, fell upon the people and lands of Egypt. In the last plague, God struck down the firstborn son in all the Egyptians' homes. Moses told the Hebrews to paint the doors of their homes with the blood of a sacrificed lamb. This was a sign to God that the angel of death was to "pass over" these homes.

When the powerful Pharaoh lost his son, he called for Moses. "Go, and take your people out of Egypt," he told Moses. The Pharaoh wanted an end to the terrible plagues.

This painting by H. Lieberman was made in 1964. It shows the waters of the Red Sea closing over the Egyptian soldiers.

Moses gathered his people together and told them they must leave at once. This hurried departure was the Exodus from Egypt. Egyptian soldiers pursued them to the Red Sea. Great winds divided the waters and the Jews passed safely across. The Egyptian soldiers were caught in the Red Sea and drowned.

When Moses and his people reached the desert, they stopped to rest and eat. They made bread dough of wheat flour and water. The bread dough, baked in the sun, had no yeast to make it rise. They called this flat, unleavened bread matzo.

Moses led his people through the wilderness. There were many hardships. When they reached their promised land in Canaan, they were at last free.

The story of being "passed over" during the plague of death and of the flight from Egypt is the celebration of freedom on the Passover holiday. The Adlers, along with Jewish families the world over, thank God for the preservation of their people.

On the first day of Passover, Mrs. Adler pours wine for the Seder dinner. The Seder is both a religious service and a grand feast. The service gives meaning to the holiday. The food and wine, as well as stories and poems, are all part of the telling of the Passover story. It is a joyous time of celebration for all the Adler family.

The wine is poured and everything is ready for the Seder. The Seder celebrates the freeing of the Jews from slavery.

Left: The cushion on which Mr. Adler leans is a sign that he can sit in the comfort of a free man. *Above:* The Seder plate holds the five important foods of the Passover.

Mr. Adler sits with a soft cushion at the head of the Seder table. He sits in the comfort of a free man, not a slave of the Pharaoh. Mr. Adler has a beautiful plate in front of him. It is called the Seder plate. On the plate are the five important foods of the Passover. There are a roasted lamb bone, a roasted hard-boiled egg, horseradish or a bitter herb, and a sweet herb. There is also a paste of fruit, nuts, and wine called *haroset*.

On the table is a special cloth that holds the flat loaves of matzo. The matzo reminds the family of the unleavened bread eaten by the Jews on their flight from Egypt. At each place setting on the table, there is the Passover book of prayers, questions, and answers. It is called the *Haggadah*.

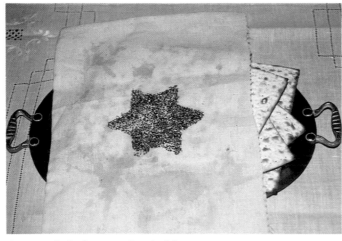

A special cloth is used to hold the matzoth.

The *Haggadah* is the book that is used for the Passover ceremony during the Seder.

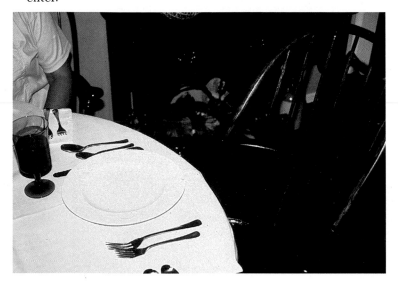

Below: An extra place is set at the table for the prophet Elijah.
Right: Mr. Adler opens the door so that the prophet Elijah can enter.

Each member of the family has a glass filled with Passover wine or grape juice. There is an extra place setting at the table, with a glass of wine and an empty chair. This place is for Elijah the prophet. The family believes that one day Elijah will come and bring peace to the world. On Seder night Father leaves the door open for the prophet Elijah.

Above: Three matzoth are placed on the table in front of Mr. Adler. They are in the matzo cloth. Mr. Adler breaks the middle one in two. He calls one piece the *afikomen. Right:* Mr. Adler hides the *afikomen* in another room. The children will hunt for it later.

The wine is blessed to start the Seder. Nathan, Sara, and Ruthie watch as their father breaks the matzo into two pieces. He calls one piece the *afikomen.* Father hides the *afikomen* in another room.

Mr. Adler reads from the *Haggadah*. The *Haggadah* tells the story of Passover. Mr. Adler reads about the time of slavery, the plagues, and the flight from Egypt. Children and adults at the table join in reading the miraculous stories.

Everyone at the Seder takes part in reading the stories of the first Passover from the *Haggadah*.

The youngest member of the family asks the four questions. These are questions about the meaning of Passover and the way it is celebrated.

Nathan, who is the youngest in the family, asks questions about the meaning of the holiday and celebration.

He asks, "Why is this night different from all other nights?"

"Why is matzo eaten instead of leavened bread?"

"Why are bitter herbs eaten?"

"Why is the food dipped twice in salted water?"

"Why is Father leaning in comfort on a soft cushion?"

The family take turns reading the answers to Nathan from the *Haggadah*. They eat pieces of matzo and taste the foods from the Seder plate.

The horseradish or bitter herb reminds them of the bitterness of slavery. The roasted lamb bone represents the lamb sacrificed at the first Passover. They taste the mixture of fruit, nuts, and wine called *haroset*. The family thinks of this as the mortar used when Jewish slaves built Egyptian temples and cities.

The roasted egg is a reminder of ancient festival offerings in Jerusalem. The sweet herbs represent the sweetness of freedom. They are dipped in salted water before eating to remind the family of the salty tears shed by the slaves.

Mr. Adler reads about the terrible plagues brought down upon the Egyptians. The family spills a drop of wine for each plague. Adult family members drink four glasses of wine during the Seder. The wine celebrates the joy and freedom in the Passover story.

One part of the Passover story tells about the ten terrible plagues that were brought down on the Egyptians.

A drop of wine is spilled as each plague is mentioned. The drops are dipped out of the wine glass with the tip of a finger.

Mrs. Adler and Grandmother have made everyone's favorite foods for the grand Seder dinner. There are fish and meat dishes and chicken soup with matzo balls, Grandfather's favorite. Ruthie's favorite Passover cake with fresh fruit is a treat for everyone.

Above left: When dinner has ended, the children hunt for the *afikomen. Above right:* Sara finds it. The reward is hers!

After dinner Nathan, Ruthie, and Sara search for the *afikomen* their father has hidden. When one of the children finds it, there is a reward. Sara looks in her favorite hiding place, and there it is! Each member of the family eats a piece of the *afikomen*. No other food may be eaten that night.

The Seder is long and unhurried. The religious service and dinner might last four hours. Seder ends after the Adlers sing their favorite Passover songs.

The Adlers follow the order of the Seder, but they can also bring their own ideas to this celebration. They have special family games. This year they have planned the Seder out-of-doors. They have acted out stories from the *Haggadah*. Passover is a family celebration, and they have the freedom to choose the way they celebrate.

Nathan, Sara, and Ruthie like Passover. They learn the history of their people through the Passover games, songs, and stories. They take an active part in this festival of freedom.

The Seder towel shown here dates back to 1821 in France. Before the head of a household says the blessing, he washes his hands in a basin brought to the table. Simple Seder towels were used as part of this ceremony. Elaborate towels, like the one shown, were used for decorative purposes.

ABOUT THE AUTHOR

For the past 25 years June Behrens has been writing for children. Her many years as an educator have made her sensitive to the interests and needs of young readers. Mrs. Behrens has written over 60 books, touching on a wide range of subjects in both fiction and nonfiction. June Behrens received her academic education from the University of California at Santa Barbara, where she was honored as Distinguished Alumni of the Year for her contributions to the field of education. She has a Master's degree from the University of Southern California. Mrs. Behrens is listed in *Who's Who of American Women*. She lives with her husband in Rancho Palos Verdes, near Los Angeles.

PASSOVER, the sixth book in the Festivals and Holidays series, is a production of the mother-daughter team of Terry and June Behrens. Terry Behrens is an ESL specialist teacher in Long Beach, California.